Integrity

Integrity

The Broken Link To Biblical Success

Dennis Cook

iUniverse LLC
Bloomington

INTEGRITY
THE BROKEN LINK TO BIBLICAL SUCCESS

iUniverse books may be ordered through booksellers or by contacting:

iUniverse
1663 Liberty Drive
Bloomington, IN 47403
www.iuniverse.com
1-800-Authors (1-800-288-4677)

ISBN: 978-1-4759-8386-9 (sc)
ISBN: 978-1-4759-8387-6 (e)

Library of Congress Control Number: 2013905720

Printed in the United States of America.

iUniverse rev. date: 8/1/2013

Table of Contents

Acknowledgements

I would like to give a big thanks to the many people who provided very valuable help in getting this cry of my heart into print.

Of course a very special thanks goes to my lovely and long time friend and helpmeet, Jeanne who has spent years in encouraging and supporting me to make this happen.

Also I want to thank the rest of my family, Christopher, Jennifer, Jason and Chad, as they allowed me to spend time necessary to bring to fruition this book.

And very importantly the many ministers of God who shared their valuable input I needed to write this.

Thank you pastors Kim Ernst, Loren Hirschy, Rich Houston and Virgil Stokes, for your encouragement and help in doing this. You all are examples of living integrity.

Introduction

For many years as a missionary serving the Lord outside of the United States of America, I have witnessed the negative effect that the lack of integrity within the Body of Christ has had on the success of the Gospel of Jesus Christ.

Each time that my family and I returned to the United States, I would scour the Christian bookstores to try and find works about integrity. With sadness I found very little on this important subject. Some of the books that I did find were out of print.

I asked myself why. Was the reason because there were few people interested in it? I know that interest for a subject plays a very important part of the decision to publish. Was it a business decision that stifled the desire to address the lack of integrity in our culture? In the Church, had we lost this vital aspect to the success of the Gospel?

Success! What is success? We need to know what God's definition of success is. How can we hit the target if we do not know what the target is or what it looks like?

Is Godly success having a new vehicle for every member of our family that drives? Is it having a big expensive home to live in or a Rolex watch on our wrist? Is it having the largest church in town or one of the biggest ministries in the country? Is it to be famous or in demand to speak at Christian conferences?

If any of these things are part of the vision that God has for you, than the answer is yes. However these things may only be an appearance of success if we are involved in building our own kingdom. If God's plan for your ministry is expressed with cars, expensive homes etc. then He will bring it about without your participation if that participation includes lack of integrity.

The accumulation of things could be used by the Holy Spirit to draw others to hear the Gospel of Salvation. However it could be used by the enemy to divert God called ministers from their God given vision. This is warned about in the third part of the "parable of the sower" in Mark chapter four where it talks about the deceitfulness of riches and how it chokes out the fruit.

Are we doing our part, to the best of our ability, to further the Kingdom of God or are we producing more firewood for a bond fire at the end of our physical existence here on the earth?

I don't pretend to know the answer to this situation existing in all aspects of our lives today including the Church. I do know that if we want true success, whether in the secular world or in the Church, we must return to the integrity of the Bible.

I felt that I needed to express the cry of my heart to encourage others with the same conviction of the Holy Spirit to continue to stand for God and His character allowing the world to see the truth of the Gospel of Jesus Christ.

I pray that all who read these pages will do so with an open heart to hear what the Spirit of God has to say and to resist the temptation to condemn those who may have fallen below the biblical standards.

May your heart be encouraged and your will strengthened as you make a decision to be whole and complete with our Father God and our Lord Jesus Christ.

CHAPTER ONE

What is Biblical Integrity?

What is the definition of Integrity? Often we have heard the word and are familiar with it but do not really know the true meaning of it. Most of us think that it is something that people in high offices or important positions have to deal with. Too often we have seen the effects of people and organizations not walking in integrity. We have seen huge organizations ruin the lives of their employees and investors because of the lack of integrity. We have even seen political decisions negatively affect a nation because of the lack of integrity. Most of the time, we don't understand that all of us should be guided by integrity. Integrity is what you do or who you are when no one else is around to see your actions.

The dictionary gives these definitions:

> A. Soundness of moral character.
> B. A sound unimpaired condition.
> C. Wholeness or completeness.

The Hebrew word for integrity thummin, means "completeness, morally innocent, perfect, or upright".

Since this book comes from a Christian perspective, we will deal with the spiritual side and how it will affect both the spiritual as well as the natural events in our life.

Basically, integrity is the measure of the internal strength of an object, whether animate or inanimate. It is what the center, the core, the heart is made of. It is what defines a person or thing and what that person or thing can be effectively used for.

Before an engineer would consider a project such as a building, a bridge or a ship, he must know the integrity or the internal strength of the building material. Whatever type of construction, it will be subject to stress and the level of integrity of the material used will be a very critical consideration.

If we were to build a house in an area, we would need to understand what type of conditions are common so that we could use material that would survive the challenge. In the Darien jungle of Panama we would not use the same material that an Eskimo would use to build a dwelling place.

I remember when we first built our cement blockhouse in the Darien jungle. Two Panamanians from the church we were attending, who had experience in building homes, accompanied me to help build our house. After clearing an area in the dense terrain we had to pour the foundation and the floor.

The area that we had picked out was on land that had never been lived on or farmed. We laid out the building lines and started digging. This was all done by hand. The plan was for a house with dimensions of 34'X50'.

After we had dug the foundation and were preparing to pour the floor, I asked why they didn't put reinforcement steel in. They said Panama did not have extreme changes in temperature and did not suffer from earthquakes. They said it was an extra expense both in time and money. Not only did they not put in any steel but also they did not even tamp the dirt before pouring the cement.

Although I did not have any experience in home construction, down in my spirit, I questioned that decision. It took us a whole week working from sun up to sun down to finish the floor. It looked really good on the surface and we returned to the city to rest.

When I returned the next week, the foundation and the floor were full of large cracks. Because we did not prepare the ground and because we did not put reinforcement in the concrete, the floor could not stand up under its own weight. We did not consider the material needed and thus paid the price.

As with inanimate objects, the level of integrity is an important consideration in a Christian leader. Can this person be trusted to pass the test? Will this person bend or break under the stress of the position? Will this individual continue to stand in his place and support the rest of the structure, church or ministry or will he twist and distort or collapse and give in to the weight of the enemy attacks?

The reason that God can be trusted in all things is that we know He is a God of integrity. He is truth. He does not change, bend or collapse. Contrary to popular belief, even in the Body of Christ, He cannot be bribed or influenced to do something different than what He has said that He would do. Numbers 23:19 says "God is not a man, that he should lie; neither the son of man, that he should repent: hath he said, and shall he not do it?"

"I am surprised at how great the mercy and love of God is for us in the Body of Christ. Why He has not killed us all and started over again is beyond me." Although we are to represent God and His character, generally speaking there is very little integrity within Christianity

We are much worse than the Israelites when they were worshipping the golden calf while Moses was up with God on the mountain. They just came out of slavery and bondage and did not have the bible to give them guidance, they did not have the indwelling of the Holy Spirit to help them know the truth, so they did tings that appeared to give them a possibility of gain and direction, but we, under the New Covenant, have no excuse.

It is no wonder that the Church has not had a bigger positive impact on the world than it has. Who can or who wants to believe in a God that supports a bunch of people lacking in integrity? Who can truly believe in people who say one thing in church and live a different life outside of church?

In the jungle we hear this comment many times from non-believers about Christians. "See that guy there, on Sunday he jumps up and down in church and speaks in tongues and on Monday he is out cheating people and lying to them. How can he be a Christian"?

I know many Christian businessmen who would rather hire a nonbeliever than a believer. What a terrible testimony for the Church. Someone somewhere said "the world is not rejecting Jesus but our representation of Him".

I remember when we first started a work in the Darien jungle of Panama with the Choco Indians. In our first village, the people made this comment to us. "We don't have a bible in our dialect but we are going to watch what you do and listen to what you say and believe that is what the Bible says to do".

I told the Lord that it was not fair. (Can you imagine me having to conduct my life like God docs? I mean live the bible!) He said that is what He wanted all of His children to be; "...a written epistle read by all men".

Without accepting the pressure, we need to understand that the world is watching and listening to us, both the good that we do and say and the bad that we do and say.

We must value integrity and character above the anointing.

How many anointed, big name ministers can we name that have fallen in our lifetime? *The anointing cannot nor will not keep you from acting like the world nor like an unbeliever.*

As J. Lee Grady, in his article in Charisma, June 2002; points out, "In the apostle Paul's guidelines for church leaders in 1st Timothy 3, only one out of the 15 qualifications listed has anything to do with spiritual anointing ("able to teach" vs. 2). Everything else in the list deals with character". We also find in Titus 1 that Paul reiterates the requirements for a leader.

Here is 1st Timothy 3:1-7 & Titus 1:5-10 combined.

1. Blameless.

2. Husband of one wife.

3. Sober or temperate (balanced).

4. Good behavior.

5. Given to hospitality.

6. Apt to teach (that he may be able by sound doctrine both to exhort...).

7. Not given to wine.

8. No striker.

9. Not greedy of filthy lucre (not given to filthy lucre).

10. Patient (not soon angry).

11. Not a brawler.

12. Not covetous.

13. One that rules well his own home, having his children in subjection (having faithful children not accused of riot, unruly).

14. Not a new Christian.

15. Have a good report of them which are without (For a Bishop must be blameless).

16. Not self-willed.

17. Just.

18. Holy.

19. Lover of good men.

Our character influences the decisions we make. In past Presidential races in the United States, there have been controversies over this very subject. It is amazing to me how so many people can be deceived into thinking that someone will make important decisions apart from their character or integrity. One of the first presidential elections that I had interest in was when a person from Colorado, Gary Hart, was running for the Democratic Party's nomination. He had not been faithful to his wife and now the politicians wanted the American people to believe that he would be faithful to the country. *Decisions are a product of our core being, our integrity, or character.* If we are not honest and consistent in the little things, we will not be honest or consistent in the bigger things.

CHAPTER FOUR

Our Response is Already Established

Remember that integrity is the material that you are made of. It is the core of your being. It is your strength to do the right thing. It is your measuring stick. It is your predetermined action in any given situation.

Godly integrity has already established our response to the temptation to walk as the world walks. Integrity gives the answer to any question of conduct. Integrity will compel a person to do what the Word of God says. It will do what is right. It will not bend to emotions of fear or greed.

When we first started working with the Choco Indians in the Darien jungle, you could place a ten-dollar bill in the middle of the village and return three days later to find the bill in the same location that you had placed it in. The reason it remained where you placed it was because of the integrity of the people. They knew that it was not theirs so they did not take it nor touch it.

Proverbs 11:3 says: "The integrity of the upright shall guide them:" This is another way of saying that your response has already been chosen when you walk in integrity. Our direction has already been provided. Follow the Word of God. Follow your heart. Psalms 119:105

says: "Thy word is a lamp unto my feet and a light unto my path..." How often has this been our prayer, Oh God give me guidance in this situation?

Many times we want God to guide us but we do not understand or accept one of the basic ways in which He has promised to do this for us. If we walk in integrity, based on the Word of God, He, through our integrity, will guide us. Remember integrity is your core material. Too many Christians are waiting on a "word" from God either through a pastor, prophet or audible voice. If we are full of the Word of God and the Spirit of God, then we already know the direction God wants us to take.

One of the basic instructions that are given to the new believer is in Romans 12:1-2 that tell us to dominate our flesh and renew our minds so that we will know God's will. It is interesting that it says that we will prove (allow, discern) God's will. The direction we need to take will be evident because we think like God. God and His Word are integral. They are one.

In other words, our integrity is a signal of the direction that God wants us to take in any given situation. We know that the scriptures do not specifically cover every possible thing but that they give us principles to help us discern the will of God for that time.

Remember, as we renew our mind with God's Word, we will begin to think like Him and will then know the direction we need to take in the situation.

How many times have we had that tug in our spirit to do something or not to do something and we ignored it? Most of us are waiting for a big booming voice to come out of the sky to give us direction or for some great prophet to give us a word of guidance. However, that is not the norm for God. Usually, those that need such are babies in the things of God no matter how long they have been born again.

I am not saying that prophets are not for today, but what I am saying is that we have looked to the wrong place for our guidance from God. 2nd Peter 1:18-19 says: "And this voice which came from heaven we heard, when we were with him in the holy mount. We have also a more sure word of prophecy; whereunto ye do well that ye take heed, as unto a light that shineth in a dark place, until the day dawn and the day star arise in your hearts:"

What is Peter saying here? He is not against a word from the Lord but he was indicating that whatever we hear must line up with the written word.

Again Paul said basically the same thing about the people in Berea in Acts 17:11. This verse says, "These were more noble than those in Thessalonica, in that they received the word with all readiness of mind, and searched the scriptures daily, whether those things were so".

We understand that although the Old Testament is the Word of God, it was written in types and shadows. In other words, when we read the Old Testament, we will not clearly see the truth of God's Word except through the light that comes from revelation of the Holy Spirit concerning Jesus and His life. **2nd** Corinthians 3:14-16 give us that understanding. It says: "But their minds were blinded: for until this day remaineth the same veil untaken away in the reading of the old testament; which veil is taken away in Christ. But even unto this day, when Moses is read, the veil is upon their heart. Nevertheless when it shall turn to the Lord, the veil shall be taken away".

Because the Holy Spirit did not reside in the spirit of man under the Old Testament, the people under this covenant did not have the advantage that we in the New Testament have. Since the Holy Spirit lives in the spirit of Christians, we can see the truth revealed through the life of Jesus Christ. When we concentrate on the Old Testament, we willingly put a veil over our eyes and that restricts our ability to understand the truth.

There is a denomination in Panama who has a unique but an unsuccessful way to evangelize. They are very good people and sold out to the things of God. They are willing to suffer hardships to reach the unsaved people of the Darien jungle.

Their approach to evangelize is to begin instructing a nonbeliever in the Bible starting with Genesis 1:1 and teaching through Malachi 4:5 with the hope that the person will understand his need for a savior before they reach the New Testament. I asked the head of this denomination what happens to the individual if he dies before he reaches Mathew 1.

I told him that the New Covenant says that it is through the foolishness of preaching that get people saved, 1st Corinthians 1:21. Although he did not have an answer, nor success in getting people saved, he did not change the approach that the denomination uses.

Most of our churches contribute in a major way to this confusion and misunderstanding of the character of God by starting both children and new converts off in Old Testament teachings. We need to get to know Jesus in an intimate way before we concentrate on the Old Testament teachings.

After all, the Bible tells us that Jesus is the exact image of God. When we know Jesus in an intimate way then we will know the true character of God the Father and will be able to discern the truth both in our lives and the Old Testament history.

CHAPTER FIVE

Integrity Will Guide, Uphold and Protect Us

The same Hebrew word for integrity, "thummim", is used to describe one of the stones in the breastplate worn by the high priest when he needed an answer from God concerning the Israelites. The breastplate of the high priest consisted of twelve stones representing the twelve tribes of Israel and two other stones called the urim and the thummin or lights and completeness, integrity or peace.

It is important to note that the breastplate was over the heart of the High priest indicating to the believer of the New Covenant that the direction of the Holy Spirit comes through the heart or spirit of man and not through the head or intellect of man. Apparently the high priest, in seeking direction for the people, would wait in the holy place near the alter of incense and before the veil, for an answer to his inquiry. God would answer him through the two stones, the urim and thummin or the lights and completeness or peace.

As we understand, the Holy Spirit rested upon only the priest, the king or the prophet under the Old Covenant. In the New Covenant, the Holy Spirit resides within the believer. This is one of the ways that the New Covenant is much better than the Old Covenant.

Today, through the revelation of the New Covenant, we understand that the believer is to wear his breastplate of righteousness as part of his attire. The Greek word for "righteousness" is dikaios and it means equity of character or act. His equity of character or act will guard his heart or spirit. The integrity of his character or actions will provide him guidance and peace in the decisions that he must make.

Colossians 3:15a reads: "And let the peace of God rule in your hearts…" In other words we are to walk and live in the light of God's Word and the peace (complete integrity or wholeness) of God's Spirit assuring us when we are walking rightly and correcting us when we are not. It is to guide us in our daily living and the decisions that we make.

Psalms 41:12 says: "And as for me, thou upholdest me in mine integrity, and settest me before thy face for ever". It doesn't matter what our circumstances may be and if people are on our side; because of our integrity, God will uphold us.

I have proven this many times in Panama from dealing with customs, immigrations or being harassed by the military or police force. Although I had to spend more time trying to accomplish something or spend time in jail, because I chose to stand with God and not pay bribes or do other things, I always came out "smelling like a rose". Because of our stand to walk in integrity we have favor with everyone from the police to immigrations.

This verse in Psalms 41 is very assuring. It will give you confidence to do what God has told you to do even if it appears that you are the only one trusting Him. A biblical example is the account of Gideon found in the sixth chapter of Judges.

Proverbs 10:29 says: "The way of the Lord is strength to the upright:" (that is those of integrity).

Psalms 37: 18-19: "The Lord knoweth the days of the upright (that is those of integrity): and their inheritance shall be for ever. They shall not be ashamed in the evil time: and in the days of famine they shall be satisfied". There have been many times that the Lord provided food for my family in a miraculous way.

I remember when we first arrived in Panama with our four children and our niece, Kathy. We didn't know anything about Panama or how to locate the lepers that God called us to help. Within three days we were pastoring a church in the American military zone about five miles from Palo Seco, the leper colony that God had shown to me in a vision.

We arrived with one thousand dollars and that amount was already decreasing. One day Jeanne informed me that we only had enough food in the house to prepare lunch. I told her not to worry. I had just finished reading a book about George Muller and his challenges with his orphanages. I told Jeanne that since God is no respecter of persons, He would provide for us just like he did for George.

At lunch time, Jeanne prepared the food that we had. After the meal, she had just a little bit left over and put it into a small pot and put the pot into the refrigerator. When dinnertime came, Jeanne approached me and wanted to know what to do.

I had expected someone to come and knock on the door with sacks of groceries. However, it did not happen and Jeanne said that she did not want to discourage my faith but the kids were hungry. Just like George, we set the table and everyone sat down to give thanks for the food. The kids looked at me and then at Jeanne with a look of "I know that mom has not been cooking and dad does not have any money to buy pizza, so why are we giving thanks.

We sat there for about an hour waiting for a knock on the door. Three times I went to look out of the door thinking the people forgot the address and were standing on the sidewalk trying to find us. I was wrong.

Finally Jeanne said that she had a little food left in the pot and that she would heat it up so that the kids could have something to eat. Jeanne took the pot out of the refrigerator and put it on the stove. When she removed the lid to the pot, it was full of food. We ate three times a day from that pot for three days. Each time Jeanne put it back into the refrigerator with just a little left over and by the next time it was full.

We knew that God had sent us to Panama. He faithfully provided all of our needs to accomplish what He sent us to do.

Psalms 84:11: "For the Lord God is a sun and shield (a protector): The Lord will give grace and glory: no good thing will he withhold from them that walk uprightly (entire, in integrity)". There are a couple of things that God has promised here, provision and protection. Even when economic times are bad, we will have sufficient supply for both the ministry and ourselves.

I remember once when there were hard economic times in the United States, whom God uses to supply the needs of the ministry. Without warning our finances declined 60%. We could personally tighten our belts but we had many obligations of the ministry to fulfill.

We started seeking God to give us wisdom and directions in this difficult time. We were able to rearrange some things to help meet our obligations. We had learned through our experience in bible school not to look to the natural for our needs to be met.

Jeanne needed a root canal done on one of her teeth. We were blessed in having favor with a Panamanian dentist and so Jeanne made an appointment to see her. When Jeanne arrived, the dentist informed her that her x-ray machine was not working and that she was going to send her to her ex-husband to do the root canal.

When Jeanne arrived at his office he was curious to know why she came to him instead of going to a U.S. military dentist to be treated.

She explained that she was a missionary and due to the treaty signed by Panama and the U.S., non-military or non-governmental personal were not eligible to receive treatment from U.S. Military sources.

Noting that this was an exceptional attitude, he asked what part of Panama she was working in, and Jeanne responded that we work with The Choco Indians in the Darien Jungle. Showing great interested in this, he explained, since childhood he has had a desire to help the Choco Indians. "I am the president of an association of professionals in Latin America who donate monthly into a fund to be used at the end of the year to help a worthy cause. May I submit your needs to the association to possibly be eligible to receive help in ministering to the Indians?" Through this non-Christian organization, just like He promised, God supplied all the needs for the ministry, until support rose back to its previous level.

Although the normal action was to try and get around the treaty restrictions, Jeanne's decision to use the Panamanian system allowed God to fulfill His word to all who choose to walk upright or in integrity in all the things big or little that come in life.

Our godly integrity will also protect from being deceived or drawn into a sinful situation that will bring consequences.

One of our missionary friends in Panama had an unregistered rifle that he kept at his house in the jungle. Although it was legal for a foreigner to have a fire arm, he had to register it and obtain a license for it. I asked him if that was wise to have this rifle without registering it or obtaining a license for it and he replied that if the government wanted to take guns away from people all they had to do was check the license registration to know who had a fire arm. He said he hought that it was wisdom to have this weapon in case he ever needed something to defend himself and his family.

A little while after this conversation I heard on my ham radio that an American living on the Caribbean side of Panama was arrest and put into prison for having two unregistered hand guns. He was retired and was legally living in Panama. He was put into prison without rights which included being able to contact the U.S. embassy. After eight months of being confined, he bribed one of the guards to let him send a letter to a friend in the U.S.

The only way that this man was released was after his friend flew to Panama with a large sum of money to buy his freedom. Had this man walked in integrity and registered his guns, he would not have suffered this terrible situation.

This illustrated the negative outcome of not walking in integrity; however I want to tell you of a positive outcome to walking in integrity.

I was a ham radio operator during the time that we began our work in the Darien jungle. There were few telephones in the jungle and those that existed usually did not work. While Jeanne and I were in Costa Rica attending a language school to learn Spanish, Noriega, the Panamanian dictator at the time, ordered a sweep of the jungle to locate illegal activities. When they arrive at our home, they found my ham radio equipment and issued an order for my arrest.

We were about to graduate from three months at this language school when we received notice of the arrest warrant. We immediately left Costa Rica to find out what the problem was. Upon arriving in Panama I went directly to the jungle to find out about this warrant. Later, the pastor of the Panamanian church that we were under, who was a judge at one time in Panama, was upset when he heard that I went directly to the jungle to confront this problem. It was common for a person to be thrown into jail and never be heard of again.

When I arrive late in the evening at the small town near our house, Santa Fe, I went to the police station and asked to see the man in charge. The attending sergeant said, "He has left for the day but he will return tomorrow. Why do you need to talk to him"? I explained that there was an arrest warrant out for me and I would like to find out the reason why. I then told the police officer that I would return the next day to talk with the man in charge. I knew the man in charge since I had spent a lot of time in his jail because of harassment.

The next day I returned and was able to speak to him. Yes he said "indeed the DENI has issued an arrest warrant for you". The DENI was like our FBI. He then went to inform the DENI agent that I was in the police station. Soon the DENI agent arrived and began to explain that he had an order to arrest me for having illegal radio communication equipment. I showed him my license issued by the government giving me the right to own and operate the communication equipment.

He then informed me that the license was good in all of Panama with the exception of the Darien province. He said I need a letter from the Major who is the governing official for the Darien Province. I showed to him that the license indicated that it was valid in all of Panama and he again insisted that in all of the other provinces it was good but not in the Darien. I needed an additional letter from the Major.

I told him that if that was true then I was going back to Panama City to the government department that issued the license and find out why they did not inform me of this. He began to say wait, wait let me contact the Major to see what he wants to do. One thing that I had figured out is when you are faced with something like this and immediately the authority does not issue a ticket or put you into custody, they are seeking a bribe.

I told the DENI official that I would return the next day to see what the Major had to say. The following day I returned to speak to the DENI agent. He told me that the Major said that I did not have to go to jail but I did need to pay a fine. I refused and told the agent that I was going into Panama City and talk to the issuing authority asking them why they did not tell me about this exception to the law governing radio communication license.

Although the agent would not return my equipment I was able to leave the police station. After the first coup attempt against Noriega, the DENI agent was transferred and also the head man at the police station. Later the new head man let me have my equipment back and confirmed that the license was valid. The DENI agent knew that I was within the law and because I followed the law, God was able to protect me from either going to jail or from being extorted.

A biblical example of this can be found in Genesis 20. Abraham tried to deceive the King of Gerar about his relationship with Sarah. Deception is a lie. Abraham was afraid that he would be put to death and Sarah be taken by the heathen King. Although what Abraham had told King Abimelech was true, it was not the whole truth. Sarah was his half sister but she was also his wife. In verses 3-6 we read how God stopped this unbeliever from sinning against Him because of his integrity. If God will protect an unbeliever from sinning due to his integrity, how much more will He protect His children from the deceptions and consequences of sin?

Not only will He sustain us, but in Psalms 41:12b we have the assurance that because of our integrity, we will be before God's face forever. This is not referring to coming into and out of His presence such as in praise or worship but about abiding, or living or being in the continuous presence of God or His manifestation. God likes to hang around people who are like HIM. It delights Him to see His people walk in integrity. Proverbs 11:20b says: "...but such as are upright in their way are his delight".

Many times our integrity gives God the opportunity to change the situation meant for our destruction around to our good and a blessing. Romans 8:28 says: "And we know that all things work together for good to them that love God, to them who are called according to His purpose". In another place, Jesus said that if we love Him, we will do what He says. We could substitute this condition of loving Him into Romans 8:28 and see that when we do what He says (walk in integrity) then that allows Him to make things work to our good. Not all things work for our good apart from the intervention of God, however we must be in agreement with or an integer with Him and His word.

In teaching about integrity in one of our Pastors Conference in Panama, we received this testimony. One of the pastors had been out of the country and had returned the night before the conference began. When he arrived home after the first day of the conference he noticed that his kids were watching Direct TV. "I knew that we did not have the finances to afford cable T.V. so after dinner, while we were all sitting around the table; I asked how we were able to connect to cable T.V."

The oldest of the kids, his son of 23 years old, responded that a friend of his at work continued to pressure him into connecting to Direct TV. "I told him no the first two times but finally I gave into the pressure. My friend assured me that he could connect the cable without any problems or fear of being caught, after all everyone was doing it".

"After listening to the explanation, I read to them from the copy of the teaching on integrity that I had received that day and then asked my children what they should do about the illegal cable T.V. connection. My oldest son said that they should turn it off. My daughter, age 18, said that they should disconnect it. My youngest son, age 11, looked up with tears in his eyes and said that they should tell the Direct T.V. company of what they had done.

The next day, we wrote a letter to the president of the cable company explaining what had happened and together with my children, we went to present the letter personally to the president. After waiting a while, we were admitted into the office of the president. We presented the letter and said that we were willing to pay for the use and accept whatever consequences that came".

The president listened and then made this comment. "I have never seen such integrity before. Although this was done illegally, because of your integrity I am going to allow you to continue the connection until the end of the year. At the beginning of next year you can either sign up and pay the monthly charge or disconnect from the service". Although it appeared to be a small thing and everyone was doing it, the integrity of this pastor brought a blessing from the company, gave a godly testimony to many people and encouraged the family of the pastor to choose integrity and blessings.

Another time when integrity protected me was when I had accidentally hit a man with my truck that I was driving.

Jeanne and I were coming into Panama City from the jungle one evening about 7:30pm. God has given me a conviction to obey the law so I was driving the speed limit at the time of the accident. As I approached a group of people walking, I noticed a child on a bicycle riding in my lane and facing my direction. On the same side and walking toward me were also other people but on the side of the road. I slowed my speed and moved to my left over the middle line to give this child room in case she fell on her bicycle. On the opposite side of the road but off the road were other people walking in the same direction as the people on the right side of the road. I made sure that I did not cross too far over into the other lane because of these people.

Approximately 40 to 50 feet behind these people was a drunken man walking right down the middle line. As soon as my headlights illuminated him, I applied my brakes and the tires were squealing as the distance between us rapidly disappeared. Although the truck I was driving was making a lot of noise, he did not look up or appear to be cognizant of the danger he faced. I hit him with the driver side front fender and sent him onto the side of the road.

I was able to stop the truck within a couple feet and quickly exited to see the condition of this individual. Although he was bleeding, he was breathing and alive. There was no communication in this area and with the help of the other people (they happen to be part of his family) we put him into the truck and raced to a hospital approximately forty-five minutes away.

After reporting the accident to the police, we waited at the hospital to see what his condition was. The police informed me that I would have to go to jail until they knew if the man would be okay or grow worse. If his condition became worse, I would have to remain in jail.

I went to the police station and filled out the report. After reading the report, the police said that because I had been truthful and because I did not leave the scene of the accident like so many others, they were going to allow me to go home before the report of the condition of the man was known.

In Panama, like many other foreign countries, judgments usually are in favor of the citizen and against the foreigner. After a trial, the judge ruled in my behalf and I was exonerated from any responsibility in the accident.

When God sees us choosing to walk in integrity, it reminds Him of His Son Jesus and of Himself. I know that when one of my children makes a decision like I would, it makes me feel very good.

CHAPTER SIX

Integrity in Our Homes and Communities

We realize that biblical integrity is not natural and it takes focused attention or discipline to be a person of integrity. We are new creatures in Christ and now should be dominated by the recreated human spirit and not by the old man, the flesh.

A man of integrity is a maturing Christian, one who is a spirit dominated person, or in other words, a person who lives according to the Word of God. He is one who is walking in the biblical light that he has.

We are the "light of the world, the salt of the earth" and ambassadors of Christ Jesus. Our desire is to please Him who saved us and not to please ourselves or other people.

It is very important for us to be conscience of our actions and the purpose of them. Galatians 1:10 reads: "...for if I yet pleased men, I should not be the servant of Christ".

We understand that Paul was not talking about displeasing people just to be mean or different. No, he was referring to when we must make a choice as to whom we will please. We must understand that God is for us and not against us. He will not ask us to do something that is not in our best interest or the best interest of His plan for our lives.

The cost of **not** walking in integrity is much more than the perceived cost of doing what is right in the sight of God. Many times we are deceived because the consequences of an action do not seem to be imminent. Due to the mercy of God, we may go for a long time before we harvest the results of our actions. God gives us time to repent of our sins and does not delight in our reaping the consequences of our wrong doing. We do not consider or think of the true cost because it may not come immediately. The cost not only to you and your family, friends and church but also to your community will come and it will be very high.

Mathew 5:13-16: "Ye are the salt of the earth: but if the salt have lost his savour, wherewith shall it be salted? It is thenceforth good for nothing, but to be cast out, and to be trodden under foot of men. Ye are the light of the world. A city that is set on an hill cannot be hid. Neither do men light a candle, and put it under a bushel, but on a candlestick; and it giveth light unto all that are in the house".

Jesus was talking to all of His disciples. Our light needs to illuminate everyone in the church or the house of God and in the world, starting with our families and communities.

As Christians, we have many chances to violate our integrity. We must operate in this world system playing by a different set of rules. The world and its followers can bend or break the rules to suit themselves, to give themselves an advantage over others. Many times it appears that as Christians we are at a disadvantage because of our integrity. We are under a lot of pressure to operate like the world.

This is really a matter of believing that God is good and that He has spoken the truth about our situation. We either believe in faith the truth of the Word of God or we believe a lie. Believing what the world has to say about a situation is to believe a lie. *Integrity is ultimately a matter of trust.*

That trust only comes by spending a lot of time with God the Father in prayer and in studying His Word. 1st John 1:7 indicates that to have fellowship with our Father we must walk in the light that we have at the time. If we choose to walk any other way than what He has indicated, then we walk in the dark.

The absence of light brings darkness. People must see that we are in God. 1st John 2:3-5 says: "And hereby we do know that we know him, if we keep his commandments. And he that saith, I know him, and keepeth not his commandments, is a liar, and the truth is not in him. But whoso keepeth his word, in him verily is the love of God perfected: hereby know we that we are in him".

As men of God, we must walk according to God's Word and not the world's system. We must mimic God and do what is right and keep our word. 1st John 2:6 says: "He that saith he abideth in him ought himself also so to walk, even as he walked".

If we promise something, then we need to have enough integrity to do it. Even if it means that we have to suffer in order to complete our word. After a short while, we will learn not to speak so quickly and freely.

In Panama it is very hard to get people to commit to something like attending a conference. They want to wait and see if something better comes along before they give their word to attend. They do not want to be bound to their word so they have learned not to give it until they are sure there is nothing that they would like better.

We can trust God because we know He is going to keep His promises. Our families and our congregations must have the same confidence in us. Don't take the easy way out and say what they want to hear just to get them off of your back. If you have promised it then do it even if it hurts.

Psalms 15:4 tell us that one of the qualities of the person who is going to dwell in God's presence is "…He that sweareth to his own hurt, and changeth not". The least you will learn is to watch what you say.

Many Christian homes lack peace because the parents lack integrity. Children are following after the world and getting into bad trouble because they do not have integrity in their homes as an example, as a guide.

Proverbs 20:7: says "The just man walketh in his integrity: his children are blessed after him". Here is a promise from God to His people concerning the future of their children. However, not walking in this principle has a negative outcome; our children will have troubles.

One reason is that they will learn how to walk without integrity. As the old saying goes, "the apple does not fall far from the tree". They will learn how to sow as the world sows and thus, reap as the world reaps.

For example: When we are driving with our children in the car and do not obey the speed limit, or we run through the stop sign, we sow seeds of rebellion into their hearts of good rich soil. When they begin to drive, guess what type of attitude that they will have for the law or those in authority. This seed will breed disrespect for all types of authority whether it is in the home, school, workplace or society.

When teaching on faith (a matter of trust) I use this example. As a missionary, I need to raise support for the work that God has us doing in Panama. This entails visiting many churches and talking to many people. I can go into a new church and meet the pastor for the first time.

After I have an opportunity to share with his congregation, he may tell me that he was strongly impressed and wants to write me a check for the ministry for $10,000. I would be excited but the next day, I would be at the bank making sure that there were sufficient funds to cover the check.

Now let us say that I have known this pastor for some years and after sharing with his church, he makes the comment that he is going to write the ministry a check for $10,000. Because I know him personally and know he is a man that keeps his word, I can put the check in my billfold and continue on my schedule knowing that when I make a deposit of that check in my bank, it will be good.

What was the difference? Both times I heard the pastor's words. One time I did not know his character and could only hope that the check was good. The other time, because I knew that he was a man of his word, I could continue on with what I had to do with full assurance that when I had time to deposit the check, it would be good.

We will begin to grow in integrity when we begin to trust God and walk according to His Word.

Remember, integrity is a matter of trust.

CHAPTER SEVEN

Integrity and Your Faith

Faith and integrity go hand in hand. If we, as a representative of God, lack integrity then it will be very difficult to have faith in God.

First we will be subject to the condemnation that our lack of integrity has allowed into our life. The devil will always remind of us of the things that were not quite right. Through this, he will attack our worthiness to receive from God.

Second, we will not be sure that God will keep His word because we don't keep ours. Integrity will give us that confidence to believe Him and the strength to continue on the path or in the direction He has given to us.

In the last part of the verse in Psalms 84:11, God tells us He will not withhold any good thing from us who walk in integrity. That fact alone will help stimulate your faith in Him and His promises.

Psalms 25:21 says: "Let integrity and uprightness preserve me;" The meaning of the word "preserve" is to guard.

Integrity will keep us from being deceived and falling into the trap of the enemy. Proverbs 2:7b: "He is a buckler to them that walk uprightly" (in integrity). If you follow God's Word in your heart, you will not fall into the traps or temptations of the devil.

I am not saying you will not have temptations and traps laid to bring you into problems, but what I am saying is that God, through your integrity, will give you a way out. Remember, God's principle of sowing and reaping is true. The harvest will come sooner or later.

Galatians 6:7-8 says: "Be not deceived; God is not mocked: for whatsoever a man soweth, that shall he also reap. For he that soweth to his flesh shall of the flesh reap corruption; but he that soweth to the Spirit shall of the Spirit reap life everlasting".

Just as an engineer who used faulty material to build a bridge or an office building may have temporarily made more money for that job, after awhile his work will show the lack of quality and future clients will not use him. Thus he will suffer for his lack of integrity both in his character and in his work. If the project collapses, he could be arrested, tried for the disaster and sent to jail for the rest of his life. The final price of his lack of integrity becomes very, very costly.

This affects not only the life of the person who lacks integrity but it also affects those associated with him, his family, his friends and the people who suffered because of his choice to take a short cut.

Every missionary that I know personally, who has paid bribes as a way of life to get favor with the authorities, is either dead or out of the ministry. They used many different justifications to pay bribes and take a short cut.

They thought that they would spend less money and time than going through the normal steps. By using bribes they thought that they could guarantee to get what they wanted the easier way. The apparent easy way is not always God's way.

Mat. 7:13-14 says: "Enter ye at the strait gate: for wide is the gate, and broad is the way that leadeth to destruction, and many there be that go in there at: because strait is the gate, and narrow is the way, which leadeth unto life, and few there be that find it".

God is a good and faithful God. He is faithful in all things. That includes protecting his sheep from deceivers.

Lucas 12:2-3 tells us: "For there is nothing covered that shall not be revealed; neither hid, that shall not be known. Therefore whatsoever ye have spoken in darkness shall be heard in the light; and that which ye have spoken in the ear in the closets shall be proclaimed upon the housetop".

As we read this scripture, we find out that Jesus is first addressing his disciples. He then talks about leaven and to stay away from the leaven of the Pharisees, which is hypocrisy.

Hypocrisy is intentionally saying one thing and doing something different. Hypocrisy is a deception both to the person who is practicing it and to the person that he is deceiving.

I know of many situations here in Panama where leaders of churches are trying to get their congregations to walk in holiness, yet they themselves are having extramarital affairs. They actually believe that their congregation is not aware of their actions.

I had a member on the board of our United Pastors group that was involved in this type of deception. He was pasturing his church in the jungle but his wife was still living in the city. She did not want to sacrifice by living without the conveniences of the big city.

One of the members of this pastor's church had a history of extramarital affairs. She began to volunteer to help this pastor out by cleaning his house and then washing and ironing his clothes. After a while, she began traveling with him to different parts of the jungle. Well, they fell into adultery.

The pastor was teaching the different churches that were either beneath him or that he preached in that it was okay to have sex with this other woman. He said that he had a need and that God was a good God and wanted to meet his needs.

I confronted him and removed him from the board of the United Pastors group. He did not see anything wrong with his actions. Everyone in that part of the jungle knew what was happening. Needless to say, it brought reproach to the name of Jesus and added excuses to the non-believer to continue to resist the working of the Holy Spirit in their life.

You know something very interesting. One of the biggest reasons that we lack integrity is because of fear, fear of failure. Fear that God will not provide for us. We are afraid that the opportunity will pass us by. Maybe we are afraid that we will have to suffer unjustly. The price that these ministers have paid is extremely high when you consider they have either died or have been taken out of the ministry.

They have left their families in shame and or financial problems. Their actions have caused many people to stumble and to not walk in faith and confidence with their Father God.

They have brought a bad testimony upon Christianity. They have been used by the enemy to bring disgrace upon the name of Jesus and His Body, the Church, here in the earth.

I know that people say that it is hard to swim upstream against the current and that life is easier by doing it the way everyone else is doing it. I believe that is why we have such good attendance at seminars that teach us how someone else did it. I am not against such seminars; I am only saying that you need to hear from God as to what to do and how.

I remember one time when we were in the U.S. looking for support. I went to a new church with a pastor that I had never met. I arrived early to spend some time with the pastor and get to know him a little bit. During the conversation, I began to comment on the popular trend at that time in Christianity. I made the comment that I did not understand why people did not spend time before the Lord and find out direction for themselves and their church.

I gave a few examples like people starting cell groups because Dr. Cho in Korea had such great success but they lost people. I spoke to him about how Larry Lee declared that the North, the South, the East and the West give up the people called to his church. When pastors tried this, they lost people. Some went on television because Kenneth Copeland had a television ministry and yet lost people.

I said that I did not understand how they could have missed the principle that Dr. Cho, Larry Lee and Kenneth Copeland had spent time in prayer and in the presence of God to find the direction that He wanted them to take. When He spoke that direction to them, they had the faith to do it and have success. Remember, "faith comes by hearing and hearing the word of God" (Romans 10:17).

Well the pastor proceeded to tell me that he had started cell groups and had lost people. He had declared to the north, the south, the east and the west to let the people go to attend his church and he lost people. He had even gone on radio and T.V. and had lost people.

Following what appears to work for others and not finding out what God wanted him to do was very costly. Well, needless to say, he did not choose to support our ministry in Panama.

I believe that it is hard to miss the blessings and protection that God has for each of us by choosing the way of integrity, the way of Jesus, the Holy Spirit and God our Father are doing it.

Just because everyone else is doing it a certain way is not a guarantee that it is God's way. In fact, it usually is an indication that it is the world's way.

Let me give you an example of something that happened in Panama many years ago. A very good Christian organization had arranged with the government of Panama to work under an educational visa to translate the Bible into the indigenous languages. Every four years the organization had to renew their visa with the government.

After many successful renewals of their visa, for some reason, the organization forgot to renew it. The government of Panama also did not remind them of their failure to renew. The organization thought that if the government was not going to say anything then they would not say anything and it would cost less to continue their projects.

Every five years Panama changes the government leaders through elections. In one of the governmental changes, a man who was against Evangelicals started to investigate this organization. He found that they had failed to renew their visa not just one time but many times.

He immediately started the process of throwing them out of Panama. They had to leave very quickly without finishing their work and without selling their property in which they had a lot of money invested.

For this lack of integrity, they lost more in money and time than if they would have obeyed the law and done things correctly.

Another result of this action was that only part of the Bible had been translated into the indigenous languages before they had to leave Panama. Many Indians have not had the opportunity to read and study the Word of God and thus not benefit from the blessings that come from being in the Kingdom of God.

How many indigenous people have suffered condemnation in hell because someone did not want to take the time and do things correctly? Or in other words, walk in integrity with God and before men.

Listen, just because someone else is not doing things correctly does not give you an excuse to not do things correctly. In the above case, the lack of integrity was encouraged because one side did not follow through and keep their obligation. The end result was devastating.

The vice president of the United States, Dick Chaney, when he was a candidate for that office in 2004, made this remark: "Water always seeks the path of least resistance and that path is always downhill".

If we seek the path of least resistance in this world's system, we will lower our level of integrity and our quality of Christian testimony. We will end up going downhill and affecting many other people in a negative way.

Lack of integrity is like anything else. It starts with the little things and before we know it we have graduated unto bigger things. It is the little fox in our grape orchard. Just like rodents that like to work either in darkness or undercover, our lack of integrity will eat away at our ability to walk upright before God and men.

I don't know if you have ever had any experience with termites but their damage on the inside of a piece of wood is usually not detectable by the untrained eye. The outside of the wood appears to be fine but under a little pressure it will give way and reveal the damage done underneath.

Tony Cooke tells this story that illustrates the dangers of taking short cuts.

In a small town in Missouri the favorite pastime was to go fishing. All of the men would meet in a café and drink coffee and talk about who had caught the biggest fish and who had caught the most fish etc.

In this same town, there lived a man who always caught the biggest fish and the most fish. Although the people would beg him to tell them his secret, he would not say anything. The people would follow him. They would try and bribe him. They tried everything to find out his secret.

One day, the town sheriff was talking to this man and asking him about the secret to his success. The man finally told the sheriff that he would show him about the secret and to come the next day and pick him up to go fishing. The sheriff was all excited and went home immediately to get his fishing gear ready for the next day.

The sheriff got out of bed early the next morning and hooked up his boat to the truck and put in his fishing gear and started out to pick up the other man at his home. When the sheriff arrived at his house, he honked his horn and waited with a lot of excitement. The man finally came out of his house wearing a coat and carrying a small hand net. The sheriff asked him if he was going to bring any other fishing gear and the man said no. The man told the sheriff that he would give him directions to the fishing spot as soon as they arrived at the lake.

After driving for a while, the man finally told the sheriff to stop and put the boat into the water. After the two men got into the boat, the sheriff headed in the direction that the man indicated. After a while they reached the middle of the lake and the man told the sheriff to stop the boat. The sheriff immediately stopped the boat and lowered the anchor and started fishing. However, the other man just leaned back and watched as the sheriff continued to fish.

After a while the sheriff asked him if he was going to fish. The man replied that he would start in a while and that the sheriff should continue to fish. After a while, the man reached into his coat and took out a hand grenade. He pulled the pin and threw it into the lake. In just a few seconds, there was a big explosion and fish began to float to the top of the water. The man took the hand net and started to scoop up the fish and put them into the boat.

Shocked, the sheriff said, "I can't believe that you would do that. You know that it is illegal to use explosives like that. You know that I am the law and that I have to arrest you for that action".

Not saying anything, the other man put his hand into his coat again and pulled out another hand grenade. After he pulled the pin, he threw it into the lap of the sheriff and asked him, "Are you going to talk or fish"?

Just like this man's actions in fishing illegally, short cuts to the things of God always lead to problems and cost a lot.

CHAPTER EIGHT

Integrity in Our Churches

Many Christian ministries do not have a good reputation because they lack integrity in keeping their promises or in the way that they conduct business in their community.

I hear many reports from unbelievers in the Darien jungle about men of God who have a bad testimony because, as a way of life, they deceive people. Ministers receive offerings in the name of one thing and use it for something else.

A very common practice, although ungodly, is for a pastor to receive an offering for a speaker in his church and then only give the speaker a small portion of that offering. The people of the congregation gave with the understanding that the entire offering was going to bless the speaker.

These same individuals use the tactics of the world system in their business dealings and in some cases treat believers worse than non-believers. They think that if there is any trouble, the Christian will forgive them and they will not have to suffer any consequences.

Deception is lying and a sign of a lack of integrity. *It is a sign of a weak relationship with God the Father.* In the eyes of the world we are hypocrites. We claim to represent a God that does not change, a God that tells the truth without deception, a God that is faithful to His word and yet we fail to keep our word and walk in truthfulness.

Luke 16:10 says: "He that is faithful in that which is least is faithful also in much: and he that is unjust in the least is unjust also in much".

When Jeanne and I were in language school in Costa Rica, I met a Canadian Baptist woman. She and her husband were getting ready to return to Bolivia to work as missionaries. He worked in the area of finances for the ministry there.

While we were in line to register, this woman began to talk about her experiences in Bolivia. She spoke about her husband paying bribes to all of the authorities. I asked her why he would want to pay bribes and break the law. She said to me, "No, no you don't understand. Everyone does it. It is a way of life.

If a person did not pay bribes, he would waste a lot of time waiting to get things done. You know "When in Rome, do as the Romans do. Besides you would be different and draw attention to yourself and stand out from among the people. You know in a foreign country you don't want to be noticed, it may be dangerous".

I asked her if that is not what we were supposed to do, be an example of godly living. People need to see us as an example to have the encouragement to stand for God and His ways. The devil has them convinced that it is impossible to swim against the current of the river. Mathew 7:13-14 says: "Enter ye in at the strait gate; for wide is the gate, and broad is the way that leadeth to destruction, and many there be which go in thereat: Because strait is the gate, and narrow is the way, which leadeth unto life, and few there be that find it".

Another thought goes through my head when I hear a Christian use that phrase about when in Rome. I think that the Romans killed the Christians so that means we should go and kill Christian also?

You know "when in Rome, do as the Romans do". I realize that the Romans do not kill Christians now but the people are referring to the actions of the Romans in the time of the Roman Empire.

In the Darien jungle of Panama we have a big tree called a quipo tree. In many areas it is the only type of tree standing. It is very big and appears to be very strong. The bark around the tree is very thick and strong but the interior or heart of the tree is very soft and weak. Many times a strong wind will cause a quipo tree to come tumbling down. The people who cut lumber know that the tree is not worth their effort to cut it down. It has no value.

Are we like the quipo tree, looking strong on the outside but weak and full of worthless wood on the inside? When the strong winds of adversity come our way, will we stand or fall under the pressure?

As we travel through the jungle, many times on foot, we become very tired and hot. The humidity is very high and many times the insects are thick. Your body is screaming to stop and rest. If you do not have the determination to fulfill the vision, you will turn back and never reach your goal. You find out what people are made of when they are under a lot of pressure either physically or mentally. Are they a quipo tree or an oak tree?

In my observations I have noticed that the victor of wars are not always the side that has the most men or the best weapons but the side that has the most determination. It does not depend on what they have on the outside; it depends on what is on the inside that brings victory.

As children of God, as members of the Body of Christ, we know that we have the best weapons. We know that we have numbers but do we have the greatest determination?

When the devil fell from heaven he only had one third of the angels with him. He cannot produce more angels or demons. Every day, the

Body of Christ is expanding; bring in more and more people to the cause of Christ.

Numbers is not the determining fact in our daily struggles here on the earth but who has the greatest determination to overcome is.

Have you ever wondered how the Christians could march singing into the Roman arenas knowing that they were going to be torn apart by wild animals? It was because of what was on the inside of them.

Unlike the quipo tree, they were solid in the inside. Because of their determination to honor God and not recant, the national religion of the eastern Roman Empire changed from heathenism to Christianity in one generation.

Is one of the reasons that we have not made a bigger impact on the world today because we lack integrity, that wholeness or completeness with God our Father?

CHAPTER NINE

Are We Profitable?

We, as leaders, (a leader is someone who influences someone else and we all qualify) must have a high enough level of integrity to be profitable to the Kingdom of God. 2nd Timothy 2:20 says: "But in a great house there are not only vessels of gold and of silver, but also of wood and of earth; and some to honour, and some to dishonour. If a man therefore purges himself from these, he shall be a vessel unto honour, sanctified, and meet for the master's use, and prepared unto every good work".

The Greek word for honor is "timé" and means value or valuable, precious, honor. It could mean profitable. However, the Greek word for dishonor, "atilmia", means dishonor, shame, disgrace or reproach.

We could read this verse like this: but in the Body of Christ there are not only vessels of gold and of silver, but also of wood and earth; some that are profitable and some that bring reproach or shame to the Body of Christ. If a man therefore purges himself from these, he shall be a vessel that is profitable, sanctified and qualified for the master's use, and prepared unto every good work.

We see that there are many types of vessels or callings in the Body of Christ but only certain ones are valuable or profitable to the Body of Christ. It makes no difference what your position or job or calling is (gold, or silver or wood or earth), the important part is if you are valuable or profitable to the Body of Christ. Notice in verse 21 that the decision to be valuable or profitable is up to you and not up to God or other people.

We understand that we all are valuable to God. He paid an extremely high price to purchase us and value is determined by the price in which the buyer or redeemer is willing to pay. I am not talking about our value to God but our value to His plan for mankind.

This means that we must make a quality decision to allow the Holy Spirit to help us overcome the flesh. He is the helper but not the doer. In other words, we must make the effort and rely on His guidance, strength and encouragement.

It is not easy since we will be changing from the "norm of this world" to the "norm of the Kingdom of God". Many people will think that you are crazy because one of the world's definitions of insanity is when someone acts contrary to the norms.

We are not crazy but peculiar. 1st Peter 2:9-12 says: "But ye are a chosen generation, a royal priesthood, a peculiar people; that you should show forth the praises of him who hath called you out of darkness into his marvelous light: which in times past were not a people, but are now the people of God: which had not obtained mercy, but now have obtained mercy. Dearly beloved I beseech you as strangers and pilgrims abstain from fleshy lust, which war against the soul; Having your conversation (behavior) honest among the Gentiles (unbelievers): that, whereas they speak against you as evildoers, they may by your good works, which they shall behold, glorify God in the day of visitation".

The lack of integrity is a sign of a weak relationship with our Father God. We know that Jesus said in John 14:21a "He that hath my commandments and keepeth them, he it is that loveth me:"

As Christians, we understand about eternal things. We understand that our purpose here is to affect this world for Jesus in an eternal way. We know that we are not continuing here in this earth only to satisfy our natural desires but that we have something much more important to do while we are still in this earthen vehicle.

CHAPTER TEN

Three Levels of Integrity

Doug Sherman and William Hendricks describe three different levels of integrity in their book, *Keeping Your Ethical Edge Sharp*.[1] As we mature in Christ, we will pass from one level to another.

A. Out of trouble level. This is "the most common level of integrity. At this level, people are motivated to be honest by fear of reprisal." However, "they feel that it is okay to get away with whatever they can." They do the right thing because they are afraid to pay the price for getting caught.

They are not doing the right thing because it is a conviction of their heart. For example: Because they do not want to lose their employment, they will do their job while their boss or supervisor is present but will be lazy or even steal things, if they are left alone. They do not think anything of taking pens, pencils, paper, envelopes etc. from the office for their personal use. They may cheat on their expense report or deceive to get a sale.

When we first moved to the Darien jungle we thought we could help the indigenous by offering them work on our farm. I had purchased and planted some hybrid corn on the farm. Compared to the normal

---

1   Doug Sherman and William Hendricks, "Keeping Your Ethical Edge Sharp" used with permission

corn that the Indians planted, the hybrid produced enormous ears of corn.

When we harvested this corn, I employed some people from one of the villages that we had a work in. I noticed that while they were harvesting they would put some of the ears into their pocket. I confronted them about this and explained that because they had not asked permission to take the ears of corn it was the same as stealing. I made them take out all of the corn that they were appropriating illegally.

After we had harvested all of the corn and the people were ready to return to their village I noticed that their pockets were bulging but not with the ears of corn, it was the seeds taken off of the ears. They thought that I would not notice their plan to get some of this corn. They thought that the opportunity was too good to pass up.

I did not confront them and allowed them to go ahead and plant the corn seeds. I knew that the seed would not produce since it was a hybrid. After a lot of work to clean the land and plant it, when harvest time arrived, the corn did not produce. They had lost a lot of time and effort along with gaining a lot of embarrassment by thinking they could get away with helping themselves to something that did not belong to them. Had they asked me, I would have gladly explained to them that they needed to get new seed to have a good harvest.

You can locate these people by their reason to do right; "I can't do this because I might get caught" or "is it worth the chance of getting caught?" The reason is not whether it is right or wrong but the possible consequences if caught.

B. Selective integrity is the second level. At this level of integrity people "decide which areas of integrity they will obey and hope their obedience to these few areas will overcome disobedience to the rest." Usually "they compare themselves to others on the basis of their strengths, but are not interested in learning about their weaknesses or in making a change."

For some people integrity is like a chair: if it's not comfortable, they won't use it.

I know a pastor in Panama who had his own small business in order to be able to supply the basic needs for his family. Among other things, he would put water in the diesel that he would sell to people to increase his income. He knew what water could do to a diesel engine but he justified it by saying it helped him earn enough money to do ministry. He felt that this small violation of integrity helped him supply the needed funds to be in the ministry. His excuse was that "everyone did it" and the reason for him to do it was to be able to work in the ministry.

You know the erroneous saying "God helps those who help themselves". If you want to rely upon the flesh and the ways of this world, then God will step aside and allow you to provide for your own needs. Remember, Mat. 18:18 that indicates that whatever we allow on the earth, will be allow in heaven.

Because of this business practice, the people would not listen to anything he had to say and used his lack of integrity as an excuse to not accept Jesus as Lord.

C. Progressive integrity. This is the third level of integrity. The people at this level are passionate in their desire to honor the Lord, doing His work, His way. They realize that biblical integrity is not natural; it takes focused attention. They know that the human heart is capable of rationalizing almost anything and have cultivated a healthy mistrust of themselves, allowing their actions to come under regular scrutiny of God's Word.

They realize that God is gracious enough to us to not reveal all the sin in our lives at once. He chooses to progressively reveal areas in their lives that He wants to conquer. Thus integrity is a path they are on. Something that is constantly changing for the better. They do the right thing because they want to honor God and because they have made it a natural part of their being.

A good example of this is the pastor who found out that his oldest son had the cable television installed in his house while he was away on ministry business. Remember how he informed the cable company and was willing to do what was right and if necessary suffer the consequences. His decision was because he wanted to honor the name of Jesus by doing right.

Remember, this comes as we mature and to mature depends on Hebrews 5:12-14 which says: "For when for the time ye ought to be teachers, you have need that one teach you again which be the first principles of the oracles of God; and have become such as have need of milk, and not of strong meat. For everyone that useth milk is unskilled in the word of righteousness (equity of character or act): for he is a babe. But strong meat belongeth to them that are of full age, even those who by reason of use have their senses exercised to discern both good and evil".[2] This is our decision not God's.

We do not want to be a part of that group Jesus was talking to in Mat. 7:21-23, "Not every one that saith unto me, Lord, Lord, shall enter into the kingdom of heaven; but he that doeth the will of my Father which is in heaven. Many will say unto me in that day, Lord, Lord, have we not prophesied in your name? and in thy name have cast out devils? And in thy name done many wonderful works? And then I will profess to them, I never knew you: depart from me you that work iniquity".

But a part of the ones who fulfill Mat. 7:24-25: "Therefore whosoever

---

2   Doug Sherman and William Hendricks, "Keeping Your Ethical Edge Sharp" used with permission

hearth these sayings of mine, and doeth them, I will liken him unto a wise man, which built his house on a rock: and the rain descended, and the floods came, and the winds blew, and beat upon that house; and it fell not: for it was founded upon a rock"

CHAPTER ELEVEN

Proverbs 6:7-23

Here is a biblical example of compromising your integrity.

Proverbs 7:6-23 says: "(6) For at the window of my house I looked through the casement, (7) and beheld among the simple ones, I discerned among the youths, a young man void of understanding, (8) Passing through the street near her corner; and he went the way to her house, (9) In the twilight, in the evening, in the black and dark night: (10) And, behold there met him a woman with the attire of an harlot, and subtle of heart.

(11) (She is loud and stubborn; her feet abide not in her house: (12) Now is she without, now in the streets, and lieth in wait at every corner). (13) So she caught him, and kissed him, and with an impudent face said unto him, (14) I have peace offerings with me; this day have I paid my vows. (15) Therefore came I forth to meet thee, diligently to seek thy face, and I have found thee.

(16) I have decked my bed with coverings of tapestry, with carved works, with fine linen of Egypt. (17) I have perfumed my bed with myrrh, aloes, and cinnamon. (18) Come, let us take our fill of love until the morning: let us solace ourselves with loves. (19) For the good man is not at home, he is gone a long journey: (20) He hath taken a bag of money with him, and will come home at the day appointed.

(21) With her much fair speech she caused him to yield, with the flattering of her lips she forced him. (22) He goeth after her straightway, as an ox goeth to the slaughter, or as a fool to the correction of the stocks; (23) Till a dart strike through his liver; as a bird hasteth to the snare, and knoweth not that it is for his life".

1. *Lack of integrity happens when the decision to do right is not made ahead of time.* Proverbs 7:6-7.

> This illustration centers on a young man (immature person) who we know is going to have trouble because he is described as simple. This is a reference to his moral immaturity. It means that he has no clear moral standards to guide his conduct. He has never made up his mind about the values he will live by. He just behaves however the conditions demand. In other words, he is a situational ethicist. He is on the fence and he can go either way depending on the situation. This is moral immaturity.

2. *Lack of integrity occurs when you underestimate evil and flirt with temptation.* Proverbs 7:8-9.

> This person is playing with fire. He is in the wrong situation and is looking for trouble. He would probably deny it though. It begins with thinking about doing what is wrong, then imagining what it would be like, and then physically placing oneself in the conditions where you might have the experience. It occurs when you flirt with temptation. It is always dangerous to underestimate evil.

3. *Lack of integrity is always just a choice a way.* Proverb 7:10-12.

> Temptation is everywhere and opportunities to violate your integrity are everywhere. After all, sin is aggressive; always waiting for you, ready to pounce (Genesis 4:7). We need to recognize that if we play with sin, it will bring us down. There are three sources of sin that may entice you to compromise your integrity.

A. "The world" or world system. It is the value system of the people around you, who do not put Jesus first in their lives or thinking. God tells us about this in 1st John 2:15-16.

B. "The flesh". Galatians 5:19-21 tells us what the flesh is capable of. There are many chances to compromise in the external environment. We must deal with our own fleshly desires.

C. The third source of evil is the devil himself. 1st Peter 5:8 tells us to watch out for the devil's tactics.

The world, the flesh and the devil are everywhere trying to lure us into sin.

Remember the trap of compromise is only a choice away.

4. *Compromise comes through flattery and fantasy.* Proverbs 7:13-17.

Nearly all temptation contains some form of flattery, even if it is nothing more than the flattery of thinking you can "get away with something." Likewise, all temptation paints a picture for our imagination, showing us how much "better off" we would be if only we would compromise our integrity. Since this young man has never made up his mind about his moral convictions and having placed himself in a situation of temptation and meeting someone or something smarter then he, he is ready to swallow the bait that will hook into the evil.

5. *Compromise ensnares through rationalization and deception* Proverbs 7:18-21.

A rationalization simply applies a good purpose to something that is inherently wrong. We all are geniuses at coming up with good reasons for bad actions. Next, evil tries to convince us that no one will know and there will be no consequences. We will reap what we sow. Even if our wrongdoing escapes the notice of our fellowmen, it never escapes the notice of our Creator.

6. *Compromise occurs with a refusal to think about the rightness of our actions.* Proverbs 7:22.

> Suddenly! Compromise is always our decision and usually it is a sudden decision. We don't want to pray, we don't want to reflect on the Word of God, we don't want to get council from our conscience, and we just do what we want to do - suddenly. If we fall into sin, it is because we choose to sin. No one makes us sin. James 1:14-15.

7. *Compromise always cost.* Proverbs 7:22-23.

> No matter how secret or private our actions, no matter how well we cover our tracks, a lack of integrity will always cost us greatly. All sin has consequences.

How does lack of integrity come? Through (1) failure to commit ahead of time to doing the right thing; (2) underestimating evil and flirting with dangerous temptations, and being exposed to far more powerful evils; (3) a failure to recognize the numerous forms of compromise lurking at every corner of life; (4) a failure to recognize the smooth flatteries and enticing fantasies of temptations; (5) yielding to slick rationalizations; (6) a sudden deliberate choice to give in to sin; and (7) a failure to consider the costly consequences of sin.[3]

---

3   Doug Sherman "Keeping Your Ethical Edge Sharp" used with permission.

CHAPTER TWELVE

Steps to Maintain Your Integrity

There was a series of photos in a magazine about José Cubera. Cubera was once one of the top bullfighters in Spain. "The photos showed how he had lanced a bull with the last and most deadly thrust of his swords, and the bull had fallen in the dust of the arena. As the spectators jumped to their feet with a roar, Cubera raised his arms to accept their thundering acclamation. The photos showed that Cubera had turned his back on the felled animal. It suddenly rallied and, in a final desperate rage, gored the proud bullfighter right through the back. Both man and beast died in a pool of blood".[4]

1st Corinthians 10:12 says: "Wherefore let him that thinketh he standeth take heed lest he fall." It can happen to anyone. Therefore, we all must stay on our guard to decide ahead of time to do the right thing, least moral compromise attacks us when we least expect it, and we fall victim to it".

Pastor Jack Hayford, in his book "A Man's Integrity", writes: "While appearing to be insignificant at the moment, seemingly minor concessions of a man's personal integrity can turn away his heart from the Lord. Things such as:

A. A slight indulgence

---

4   Pastor Jack Hayford "A Man's Integrity"

B. A white lie.

C. A passing flirtation.

D. A small compromise.

E. An adjusted dollar figure.

F. An unpaid stamp or office resource.

G. An inaccurate expense report.

H. An accepted gif for a special service (a bribe).

The violation of our heart's integrity can disqualify us from "running our race" faithfully with God 1st Corinthians 9:24-27

I read a simple illustration of this. A pastor said that in his desk he had many pens; but that one section in his drawer was for pens which no longer worked. They were no longer able to write or function properly, having been dulled or broken through misuse or uncleanness. When asked why he kept the pens that didn't work, he noted that they were either gifts from loved ones or commemorative pens from special events. Although he kept them, they were valuable to him even though they didn't write, but they had become "disqualified" for use.[5]

How you handle it when you blow it is as much a part of your integrity as not doing wrong in the first place. Sometimes you have to choose whether you are going to be a fool before men or before God.

Here are some steps that you can take to help maintain integrity.

A. Be honest. Don't cheat or steal:

1. Time at work. Give a good day's work for a good days' pay.

2. Energy theft on the emotional level. Allow non-work interest to distract you from the job, from your marriage, or your family.

---

5   Pastor Jack Hayford "A Man's Integrity"

3. Cheating on expense reports.

4. Use of company long distance line for personal calls.

5. Stealing supplies from work or using the copier for personal things without paying for them.

6. Violating copyright laws through illegal copying of computer software, music, videos etc.[6]

As owners of the first and only Christian radio station in the Darien jungle we are presented regularly opportunities to violate copyright laws. Many people, including ministers, will ask us to make copies of music for them. They do not have abundant monetary resources and use this as a justification to violate the law. I explain that when a person copies a tape or CD without permission it is the same as robbery. God has given to the artist or minister this method of supplying their needs both for their ministry and for their personal lives. Coping without permission is robbery.

B. Obeying authority. All legitimate authority is from God. 1st Peter 2:13-17 says: "Submit yourselves to every ordinance of man for the Lord's sake: whether it be to the king, as supreme; or unto governors, as unto them that are sent by him for the punishment of evildoers, and for the praise of them that do well. For so is the will of God, that with well doing ye may put to silence the ignorance of foolish men: As free, and not using your liberty for a cloke of maliciousness, but as the servants of God. Honour all men. Love the brotherhood. Fear God. Honour the king".

Yielding to such authority is an expression of yielding to God's authority.

1. Submit to the government. Romans 13:1-7. We must always obey laws that are clear and unequivocal. When

---

6   Pastor Jack Hayford "A man's Integrity"

rules and regulations are unclear, it is important to seek professional as well as biblical wisdom. Our tendency is to make decisions on the basis of only how it benefits us, not what is fundamentally the right thing to do. We need the objectivity of others

2. Submit to your employer. Colossians 3:22-24 says: "Servants, obey in all things your masters according to the flesh; not with eye service, as men pleasers; but in singleness of heart, fearing God. And whatsoever ye do, do it heartily, as to the Lord, and not unto men; knowing that of the Lord ye shall receive the reward of the inheritance: for ye serve the Lord Christ".

    The way that we relate to our boss and the authority structure at work is ultimately the way we relate to Christ's authority.

    How we relate to authority has a direct bearing on our testimony for the cause of Christ. Titus 2:9-10.

C. No deception. Deception is a form of lying and God hates lying. Proverbs 12:23.

D. Sexual fidelity. None of us is above committing sexual immorality. Here are some ways to help remain true.

1. Make up your mind that sexual immorality is wrong and that sexual purity is right. If you are married and you are sexual with anyone who is not your spouse, you are sinning.

2. Decide that you will fulfill your sexual needs in a healthy

way in marriage. Decide that marriage is the only relationship in which you will have sexual intimacy.

3. Watch out for overwork and emotional exhaustion.

4. Take care for where your need for significance and emotional intimacy is met.

5. Don't flirt with danger.

6. Watch what you watch.

7. Set high standards for your dating relationships.

8. Safeguard yourself against temptation.

9. Pray that you will maintain your sexual purity.

10. When you face temptation flee. 2nd Timothy 2:22.

11. Never forget the consequences of Immorality[7].

E. Trustful. Most people make contingency commitments.

They will agree to something until something better comes along. In Psalms 15:4 we find that one of the characteristics of a person of integrity is that "he swears to his own hurt, and does not change."[8]

---

7   Pastor Jack Hayford "A Man's Integrity

CHAPTER THIRTEEN

Grey Areas

In short, biblical trustworthiness means that when I am given a task or when I commit to doing one, I follow through on the assignment to the best of my ability, sticking with it until it is done and done right. If that is not a part of my style of work, then I really cannot say that I am a person of integrity.

Our trustworthiness is a good measure of our spirituality. The extent to which we follow through on our commitments says volumes about our fundamental commitment to Christ.

Partial obedience is no obedience.

What should we do when it seems that there is no right answer? We all know that the majority of choices are in what we call the "gray areas". Areas that is not completely right or completely wrong. How do you maintain your integrity when you are dealing with these "gray areas"?

1. Know the Bible and commit yourself to obeying it. There are four levels on which the Bible can relate to issues that you face.

> A. The first level is prohibitions: instructions that are clear and straight forward, apply directly to specific areas of life,

and are stated mostly in the negative, in terms of what you must not do.

B. The second level has to do with the positive commands. These are easy to understand and speak to broad, gene of behavior.

C. The third level of biblical instruction is values and principles.

D. The fourth level is the area of conscience.

2. Look for principles in scripture, not just commands. Principles are basic truths taught by the Bible that apply to life. Whatever principles that you find need to be consistent with the rest of the scriptures.

3. Use Bible principles to determine how you should respond to moral situations.

4. Listen to your conscience. A morally mature person is one whose conscience is healthy and well developed, having fed itself on the Word of God. Hebrews 5:14.

5. If everyone else is doing it, watch out! In ambiguous situations, it is a good bet that the crowd will generally sick together and be wrong. Integrity of heart is the result of a man who will (1) keep tuned to the voice of the Holy Spirit's correction prompting his soul, and who will (2) keep wholly, completely, entirely dependent upon the Lord.

Integrity is largely the product of growing intimate with God.

1. People become intimate with God as they open themselves up to Him.

2. People who become intimate with God center their understanding of God and His will around the Bible.

So avoid knowing only the Book, and go on to know the author of the Book intimately.

3. People who become intimate with God do so because their relationship to Him is nourished frequently and goes on continually.

It is important to surround yourself with people of the same mindset, someone that will hold you accountable to a life of integrity. The world is constantly bombarding your mind with temptations to do things the world's way. The opportunities to compromise are all around us and without the support of others we will yield to this disintegration of the godly character in our spirit.[9]

---

9   Pastor Jack Hayford, "A Man's Integrity"

CHAPTER FOURTEEN

Impact of Our Integrity

1. The impact of integrity on ourselves and our faith. There are many but one is a sense of dignity and self respect when our lives are clean before God and man. 1st Timothy 1:5 says: "Now the end of the commandment is charity out of a pure heart, and of a good conscience, and of faith unfeigned (sincere, without hypocrisy):"

2. The impact of integrity on our families. Our children have hearts filled with good rich soil waiting for godly seeds to be planted into them. Proverbs 20:7: "The just man walketh in his integrity: his children are blessed after him". However, Proverbs 15:27 says: "He that is greedy of gain troubleth his own house;"

3. The impact of integrity on people around us. It can create a moral climate to encourage others to do the right thing, even those that are not believers. Mathew 5:16: "Let your light so shine before men, so that they may see your good works, and glorify your Father which is in heaven".

4. The impact of integrity on our relationship with God. In Psalms 15 remember where David ask the Lord "Lord, who shall abide in thy tabernacle?" In other words, who

gets to be close to God? Well, the answer is clear, "He that walketh uprightly, and worketh righteousness, and speaketh the truth in his heart".

5. The impact of integrity on the cause of Christ. While people in our society are still coming to salvation, they are not doing so at a rate that keeps pace with the growth of the population. One reason is the loss of integrity on the part of so many believers. Titus 2:9-10 instructs us to have a way of life that will make the gospel attractive.

As a pastor friend of mine, Rich Huston says, "the reputation that your ministry has is in direct proportion to your level of integrity. Integrity and honesty are inseparable. If you want to be a great person of integrity, be honest with God, be honest with yourself and be honest with others".

Mathew 25:14-30 tells us about three men given responsibility by their master. Eventually he reviewed their work and rewarded them accordingly. What we do now will be evaluated by Him in Heaven someday, and that means there are eternal rewards or consequences to our earthly behavior, even as Christians. Our ultimate salvation won't be on the line, but some aspect of the life we live with God for eternity will be affected. 2nd Corinthians 5:10: "For we must all appear before the judgment seat of Christ; that everyone may receive the things done in his body, according to that he hath done, whether it be good or bad".

CHAPTER FIFTEEN

Your Day in Court

Both in the natural and spiritual realms there are consequences and rewards for the work we do and the way we do it. In the natural realm, there are many things that a person can employ to try and change the outcome of an action or series of actions. The natural realm is subject to influence and change. We can all recall a decision or result of something that seemed unfair.

Unlike the natural realm, there will be ultimate, eternal rewards or consequences as we stand before Christ. Due to the unchangeable character of our Father God, there will be no excuse or outside influence to alter the recompense of our actions during our time on earth. We will not be able to give the excuse that we were trying to help the cause of Christ. We will not be able to offer imperfect sacrifices to our God.

Jesus said, "if you love me then you will do as I say". Will someone marry a person who does not love him or her or someone who is not on the same page?

The principle is one of accountability. One of the temptations of the last days will be to forget or try to avoid the principal of accountability. We can see this lack of accountability at all levels in our society today.

It seems that the 60's generation as well as the proceeding generations has tried to live a life without rules, or what are called norms, to guide them in their conduct. We can see the result of this type of attitude by looking at the history of other powerful empires or nations. It is a true saying that those that do not know history are bound to repeat it.

Biblically there are different judgments. Although our nation will be judged by what it does on the national, state and local level, we too will be judged on an individual level.

I know many people who deceive themselves by professing that ignorance will give them a way of escape. I have heard many different justifications used when integrity was not exercised. Excuses from "God knows that I am weak in this area" to "I can't allow this thing to continue and affect others negatively".

Many times we think that our convenience is enough justification. In approaching situations through our own abilities, manipulations or sources, we are depending upon the arm of the flesh. I am not trying to cause fear but want to help people realize the importance of personal integrity.

We will be held accountable for the way we have lived. Knowing that we will look directly into the eyes of the One who bore all of our sins and knows us through and through and that He will look back into our eyes to pronounce on our earthly existence, both the good and the bad done in our body, ought to make a radical difference in us right now.

When I stand before Jesus my Lord and Savior, I want to know that the reflection that I see in His face is that of a smile and not a reflection of the big bond fire that is behind me, burning up my works.

Mathew 25:21 which says: "And his lord said unto him, well done, thou good and faithful servant: thou hast been faithful over a few things, I will make thee ruler over many things: enter thou into the joy of thy lord".

I want to see people in heaven because they accepted the message God sent me to share as an ambassador of Christ. I do not want to hear the cries from those in eternal hell that were negatively affected by my worldly actions.

Proverbs 10:9 says: "He that walketh uprightly walketh surely".

CHAPTER SIXTEEN

Can God Count on Us?

Pastor Jack Hayford made a comment in a book that he wrote on integrity. He mentioned that he has had the opportunity to address perhaps one half million pastors in his lifetime. One question he continually receives is, "What is the key to your success?" He stated that basically people want to know the number of hours that he prays, or reads the bible, or prepares his messages etc.

Pastor Hayford discerned their idea of what God was interested in was works. However, the truth is that God is most interested in man's heart. Integrity involves being complete, entire and total. God is interested in the integrity of our hearts. He wants us to live like Him, be a reflection of His character on this earth. He knows that if we walk in our integrity of heart, produced by our strong relationship with Him, we will have great success.

Can God count on us? Do we have the inward strength to walk in integrity? Do we have a relationship strong enough to stand on God's side when the tough times come?

Both the world around us and the people with us are observing and depending upon us to demonstrate God's will and character.

Will we show that His ways are better? Can the people that God has given to us to serve trust us to pass the test?

Just as God the Father, God the Son and God the Holy Spirit are one in purpose and direction (an integer); let us determine to walk as one in the Body of Christ, in our families, in our churches and in our ministries.

1st John 2:6 says: "He that saith he abideth in him ought himself also so to walk, even as he walked".

Let us allow our integrity to produce the godly results promised in the Word of God. Let it guide us, protects us and allow us to walk in God's presence continually.

About the Author

Dennis and Jeanne Cook and their family have been missionaries to the Republic of Panama since November, 1981. They have four children, Christopher, Jennifer, Jason and Chad who were vital in the early success of ministry. Jennifer is their United States office manager and Chad is still ministering with them in the Darien jungle. Christopher and Jason provide financial and logistic support to the ministry.

Both Dennis and Jeanne graduated after two years training from Rhema Bible Training Center in Broken Arrow, Oklahoma. After spending their first two years in Panama ministering in a leper hospital located beside the Panama Canal, the Holy Spirit led them to the Darien jungle to minister to the Choco Indians. The Darien jungle is the largest province in Panama with the least population due to the density of the jungle and its boarders with Colombia.

Along with establishing churches in Indian villages they have the first and only Christian radio station broadcasting in Spanish to the entire province of Darien. Their goal is to transmit in the four major dialects that are represented in the Darien jungle.

For ten years they conducted conferences in Panama City for pastors, their wives and children. They now conduct these conferences for pastors and their wives in the jungle as well as other Central American countries, Colombia and Brazil.

To contact the Cooks for scheduling or donations visit our webb site: vidaministries.fatcow.com